How to Obtain a Place

How to Obtain a Place in Medical School

W. GRAHAM WESTALL

General Practitioner
Cardiff

LONDON
Chapman and Hall

First published in 1984 by W. G. Westall
Second edition published in 1987 by Chapman and Hall Ltd
11 New Fetter Lane, London EC4P 4EE

© 1987 W. G. Westall

Printed in Great Britain by
J. W. Arrowsmith Ltd, Bristol

ISBN 0 412 29750 7

British Library Cataloguing in Publication Data

Westall, W. Graham
  How to obtain a place in medical school.—2nd ed.
  1. Medicine—Vocational guidance.
  I. Title
  610.69   R690

ISBN 0-412-29750-7

To my wife, Janet,
for all her patience and
encouragement, and my sister, Barbara,
who has so kindly typed and
re-typed the manuscript.

Contents

Preface

This manual is for the aspiring student of medicine. You have a keen desire to study the fascinating story of how the human body works and what to do when things go wrong. You want an occupation where you can help other human beings, and also receive a respected and trusted position in society. You realise that in addition you will be paid an above average income, and have good job security. Perhaps you were attracted to medicine by the treatment you received when you, yourself, were ill in hospital. Maybe you watched a television programme on medical matters and this aroused your interest. Perhaps one of your parents or another relative is a doctor and that is where your interest in medicine originates. Possibly, your religious faith prompts you to enter the healing profession, and you may even have leanings towards becoming a medical missionary.

This publication is intended to enable you, the average student, to get your feet on the first rung of the medical ladder, namely, a place in a medical school. Don't be fussy! It is an achievement, in these competitive days, to obtain a place in any medical school. Unless of course you are brilliant, like one acquaintance, who was personally congratulated by a telephone call from Cambridge University when he obtained his outstanding Advanced Level examination results. This book contains advice on how to get into medical school. Some fact or piece of advice here might make all the difference when you are trying to obtain that vital place. One chapter contains hints on how to make the most of your time when you arrive at university.

What are the author's qualifications? They are modest, in fact. At
the age of about twelve, he decided that there was no other
vocation for him. It was to be medicine and nothing else. After that
momentous decision he proceeded to pass, at first attempt, all the
usual school and University examinations. Naturally, like any other
student, the author became aware of much useful information
along the way, which he passes on to you in this book. You are
wished every success in obtaining that coveted medical school
place.

   One initial piece of advice. Don't let the medical schools know
that you have read this book. Professors and deans are averse to
those who practise one-upmanship.

1
Getting down to realities

Recently, the author attended a reunion meeting with some of those students who commenced studying medicine with him at Bristol in 1957. It was interesting to look back on those days when entry to medical school was relatively easy. The number of medical school places was approximately matched by the number of applicants with the required Advanced Level passes. Nobody worried about grades. Medicine then was not such a glamorous or popular subject, and in any case, a place at medical school could be obtained with quite modest Advanced Level passes in three subjects – or even in just two subjects in a few fortunate instances. As we chatted together at the reunion, we talked about how fortunate we were to have obtained a place in medical school. Today, many of us would not have had the chance to study medicine. Yet, some of those attending are prominent members of the medical profession. It used to be said (by physicians, I think) that it was possible to become a consultant orthopaedic surgeon with an intelligence quotient of 100. Even if that were ever true, it certainly would not be today.

So we must get down to reality. Medicine has become a very popular university course. A typical London medical school will have more than twenty applicants for each place. Yet courses in veterinary medicine attract even more hopeful applicants. Paradoxically, your household pet will, in future, be handled by the 'intellectual cream'. It now costs approximately £100 000 to train a doctor. During the last decade or so, it has become increasingly difficult to obtain a medical school place. Now every year some

6000 disappointed students are turned away, and have to look at other university subjects or occupations. This can be a shattering experience for many applicants to medical school. Today, subjects like chemistry and biology no longer offer such good job prospects at the end of the degree course. This may have resulted in an increasing number of pupils looking towards medicine for their career of choice. If you are keenly motivated and 'vocational' in your attitude to medicine, the thought of the keen competition may freeze you into feeling that you will never obtain a place in medical school, especially if you are of average academic ability. In fact these desirable qualities themselves may make you excellent material to train in medicine and become a successful consultant or general practitioner. The tortoise usually beats the hare in the long race.

One of the problems that you will face in trying to obtain a medical school place is the attitude of the dean. This is the all-powerful man (usually) at each medical school, who has his thumb on student selection. The dean's job is, admittedly, a very difficult one. For example, at Newcastle the dean may receive some 2800 applications for a mere 150 places. Some medical school deans seem to take the easy option and select on Advanced Level grades only. Elsewhere, the dean will make every effort by means of interviews, school reports, personal reports etc. to obtain as much information as possible about applicants. Some deans will be most interested in your hobbies and interests. The dean at one provincial medical school was reported in 'World Medicine' as saying that he believed a prospective student's outside interests were of no importance! At Leicester, however, the dean seems fully aware that Advanced Level grades are uncertain indicators of a student's subsequent career. Medical schools now take more female students. This is undoubtedly a reflection of the more independent role of women in society. Recently, 55% of first year students at the University of Wales College of Medicine were women.

Imagine for a moment the dean's dilemma at the average medical school with only 150 places available and almost 3000 applications arriving from the Universities' Central Council on Admissions. From October onwards, every year, the dean and his assistants receive about 2–300 applications *every week* and this continues until January or February when the numbers decline. The applications contain basic facts about the pupil's Advanced Level potential, together with a confidential report from the head teacher. Each pupil will have probably applied to four other medical schools. The problems of the dean are enormous. How can he find the 300 or so applicants to whom he can make a provisional offer for the 150 places? (50% of those offered a place will either fail to get the required examination grades, or else having obtained high enough grades, will opt to go to another medical school which has also offered them a provisional place.) No dean can fail to accept a pupil who has received an 'offer' and who then subsequently obtains the desired Advanced Level grades. The lower the grades required, the fewer are the provisional places that can be offered. For example, if the medical school requires CCC grades, then that dean can only afford to offer say 250 places. If the medical school requires BBC grades for admission, then it could make 350–400 offers of places. Medical schools who exceed the intake allotted by the appropriate government department could face punitive measures.

All aspiring medical students apply through the Universities' Central Council on Admissions (UCCA). The way in which you complete the UCCA form is all important and will be discussed at length in Chapter 4, which deals with UCCA application procedure in general. Normally, you would apply to UCCA in the autumn term of the year before which you intend to enter medical school. Make sure you obtain the prospectus from as many medical schools as possible, and thus obtain the facts about the required Ordinary and Advanced Level subjects. Many Universities will require the applicant to pass a foreign language at Ordinary Level. Latin is no longer required.

So you can see that there are at least two major obstacles in your way before you can start studying medicine. The *first* obstacle is that of obtaining a provisional medical school place. This is called a 'provisional offer'. The offer depends upon your being able to obtain a certain level of grades in the Advanced Level examinations which you will be taking some months after you have been provisionally accepted. The *second* obstacle is probably the greater. You will have to deliver the goods. You must obtain, in almost every case, at least the requested grades. If you fail by the smallest margin to obtain those grades, you will be extremely unlikely, because of stiff competition, to be given your desired place. But don't let this depress you. This book will help to clear those two obstacles, difficult as they may be. Forewarned is forearmed.

At this stage, it may be useful to mention the possibility that medical schools are producing too many doctors. There are, at present, an estimated 3000 unemployed doctors in Britain. There could well be more than this. Nobody knows for certain. Unemployed doctors are usually most reluctant to disclose their status. Possibly they feel that this would not help their professional image. People could ask, 'How can a good doctor be unable to find a job?'. For similar reasons, unemployed actors usually tell you that they are 'resting' between jobs. It is possible that in the future a few unfortunate and unemployed doctors could, in desperation, be willing to become sales representatives for a drug company, i.e. they would visit doctors in hospital or general practice and seek to promote their employer's drugs. PhD's in science subjects are already doing this. For a medical graduate to end up advertising drugs does seem to be a waste of the £100000 needed to educate him or her.

However, there always will be a demand for able doctors to work hard in the National Health Service or elsewhere, and opportunities are always available in overseas countries. Whilst British doctors are now scarcely needed at all in Australia and North America, there is plenty of scope in the Arab and Third World countries. If you can speak a European language, the EEC countries will offer you the chance to practise – usually without the need to take further post-graduate examinations. Anyway it is extremely difficult for the Department of Health, the British Medical Association, or any other body to predict just how many doctors will be required in the United Kingdom in ten or twenty years' time. It takes some five years to train a doctor and this does not help those bodies who are trying to predict the future need for doctors. In addition, disease patterns change and new diseases appear. Medical specialities constantly fragment and form sub-specialities and more doctors are absorbed into these new areas. How many doctors will find jobs because of the AIDS outbreak? Nobody can foresee how many doctors will be employed in private practice in twenty or thirty years' time. Assuming that 50% of medical school places are now taken by women, nobody knows how many of these will either give up practising medicine or practise only part-time in future. At present, a general practitioner can continue working in the NHS until he is ninety years of age! This might well be changed, and many elderly general practitioners would then leave at sixty-five years of age or even earlier if inducements were made, or if seniority awards were removed at sixty-five.

In the late 1950s, the Willinck Committee reported on the

number of doctors required in the UK. It was suggested that we were training too many students so that their numbers were reduced by 10% or so. One result of this incorrect arithmetic was that through the 1960s, provincial hospitals had to rely heavily on foreign graduates, (especially from India and Pakistan) to fill junior hospital posts. There were simply not enough home-grown doctors to fill these vacant posts. Many of these foreign doctors had great difficulty in conversing in English with unfortunate patients who had equal difficulty in making themselves understood. Now, the government is placing an increasing restriction on doctors from overseas wishing to practise here – rather like the USA did years ago. This will have the effect of increasing the job market for British graduates.

So take heart! You will be able to find a job if you work steadily and conscientiously and keep your options open. It would, of course, be unwise to set your heart on becoming a consultant cardiac surgeon and nothing else. Britain might require only a mere handful of these specialized doctors, at the most, each year, and promotion is very slow. When you eventually attend for medical school interview, don't be afraid to say, in reply to questions asked, that you are keeping an open mind and don't yet know in which area of medicine you will work. At least the interviewers will know that you are a realist, and will not smile after you have taken your leave of them.

2
Digging
the foundation

Your first academic requirement to enter medical school will be the possession of an adequate number of passes in Ordinary Level GCE subjects. At least seven passes will be required if you are to attract the notice of the medical school selection committee who will not have your Advanced Level results available when they first scrutinize your UCCA application form. You will need good grades at Ordinary Level (mainly As and Bs) especially in those three subjects which you will be offering at Advanced Level. Indeed, think twice before embarking at Advanced Level on a subject in which you have failed to gain an A or B grade at Ordinary Level. An A grade in an Ordinary Level subject is a confidence-booster for the pupil commencing Advanced Level studies in that subject. At Ordinary Level, chemistry is usually essential and physics, biology and maths are strongly desirable. A pass at Ordinary Level in one foreign language is also usually needed.

CHOOSING YOUR ADVANCED LEVEL SUBJECTS

As soon as you have received your Ordinary Level results, you will need to start consulting medical school prospectuses which can be obtained from the dean of that medical school. Then you can check whether your preferred medical schools require any particular subjects at Advanced Level. This is most important because the appropriate Advanced Level passes will place you in the second year of the six year medical course which is already long enough. (Few medical schools now operate a first year course which is known as the first MB course.) The normal Advanced Level subjects that you would be wise to consider are chemistry (nearly always essential at most medical schools) with, in addition, any two from the following: physics, biology (or zoology,) or maths. The maths may be pure and applied maths as one subject, pure maths, applied maths, or pure maths with statistics, etc.

When selecting your Advanced Level subjects, consider carefully which three subjects would give the greatest chance of a good grade at Advanced Level. You would be wise to take into account the 'strength' of the various departments in your school or college. Ask yourself: 'Does the teacher in that particular subject have a good pass rate amongst his Advanced Level students?' You are entitled to obtain the results of the previous year's Advanced Level examinations for a particular school from the Local Education Authority. Is your teacher inclined to be 'exam-orientated' and likely to drive you 'hard'? Does he/she have your interests at heart and realize how keen you are to gain those Advanced Level examinations in order to commence medical studies? If you have any doubts, you might consult the previous year's pupils. In some schools with mediocre sixth form courses, you might be better to consider studying your Advanced Level subjects at another state school, a college of further education or even at a private school or college if your parents' funds permit! This may mean leaving your friends at the local school, but it may make the difference between obtaining a B grade or a C grade at Advanced Level. Incidentally, in some Advanced Level subjects, there may be as little as 3% (total mark) difference between a B grade and a D grade. If you have already started in the lower sixth and are not satisfied with your teachers, you will have to make an early decision as to whether you will need to change to another school or educational establishment. Obviously the longer you leave this move, the more difficult you will find it to integrate into the new college or school. Get as much advice as possible about this. It is the author's opinion that many medical school applicants have had their prospects ruined by a poor Physics teacher.

ADVANCED LEVEL SYLLABUSES AND EXAMINATION BOARDS

The Advanced Level examinations of the various examination boards around the United Kingdom are supposed to correspond with each other in the degree of difficulty of their various examinations. In other words, a pupil who can only obtain a C grade at the Welsh Joint Education Committee examinations would only, presumably, obtain a C at the Oxford local examinations. This not only sounds unlikely, but it is. Teachers also dispute the equality of the various Advanced Level GCE examinations. One examiner told me recently that his employing examination board set easier papers in his subject, than did his local board. On the other hand, different groups and standards of pupils are entered for the Advanced Level examinations at the various examination boards. How do you compare results from an examination board that tests mainly public school pupils (with a good teacher/pupil ratio) with an examination board whose catchment area is working class and where comprehensive education is the norm? (You will find the addresses of the examination boards in England and Wales in Appendix 3.) The Oxford and Cambridge Board is said to have a higher pass rate than the Associated Examination Board, but the former examination board will have a high proportion of pupils from public schools and 'crammers' amongst its examinees. The Associated Examination Board serves a much wider educational population. Incidentally, the medical school dean is not particularly interested in any particular examination board. He is only concerned with the grades that you obtain.

Normally at Advanced Level, the top 10% of candidates will achieve an A grade. The next 14% will attain to a B grade, and the next 12% will receive a C grade. So, roughly speaking, to obtain an A, B, or C grade you will need to be in the top one-third of candidates and to obtain an A or B grade, you will need to be in the top quarter of the candidates. This gives you an idea of the competition which you are facing.

If you have time, send for a syllabus and specimen examination papers from each of the examination boards. Then, whilst you are beginning to study your Advanced Level subjects, try to decide if your own local examination board seems to be asking the most reasonable questions. If not, consider sitting the examination papers of a different examination board. I strongly suggest that you obtain an Advanced Level syllabus for each of the three subjects which you are taking. Then, as you prepare for your Advanced Level examinations, you will be able to tick off, on the syllabus, the various topics as you consider them. In that way no part of the syllabus can be overlooked and thus you will not be reducing your chances of being able to tackle all of the questions.

The GCE Advanced Level syllabus (or regulations)

At this stage, it is worth giving further attention to the syllabus, a copy of which your Advanced Level examining body will be able to provide for you at the cost of a pound or so. This document will outline, for each subject, the course of study. It is with this framework in mind that the chief examiner will compose the written questions and practical tests. When you first see the syllabus for your Advanced Level subject, you may naturally be overwhelmed! The range of topics to be studied seems so wide. But don't shake at the knees! You will cover this course of studies gradually and there will be overlap between the topics to be studied in each subject. Sometimes there is even overlap between different Advanced Level papers, for example, the mechanics section of the physics paper will overlap, to some extent, with the applied maths paper. Therefore it is obviously an advantage to study these two subjects, at Advanced Level, together.

Using the syllabus

Whilst your teachers are taking you through the course of Advanced Level studies, you should pause from time to time to distinguish the wood from the trees. In other words, see just what section of the course you are supposed to know and which sections are still outstanding and will still need to be studied. It may be that your teacher's enthusiasm may lead him or her into topics about which you will never be tested. That's fine if you are brilliant, but if you are short of studying time, and find the subjects difficult anyway, there is no point in delving into matters on which you can never be specifically questioned.

May I illustrate what I have said in the preceding paragraph. The author found physics to be a difficult subject to master, especially since his knowledge of maths was limited to Ordinary Level standards. Our excellent, enthusiastic school physics teacher was keen to spend time on matters about which the Welsh Joint Education Committee course stated: 'A knowledge of this will not be expected'. I do remember that this good teacher was a little grieved, to say the least, that we prospective medical students were 'working to rule' and were keen to have a good grasp of only those areas of the subject in which we could possibly be tested. He did not

seem to understand that our thirst for knowledge was satisfied with
the topics described in the syllabus.

OLD EXAMINATION PAPERS

The examination board's syllabus is a type of meeting point
between the examiner and yourself. I imagine, though I can't prove
it, that apart from a biro, the chief examiner has two things near at
hand when composing those questions that are to be tackled by you
some eighteen months later – firstly, there will be a copy of the
regulations on the desk, and secondly, a bundle of old examination
papers from the examiner's own examination board and probably
from most of the other examination boards as well. Make sure,
therefore, that you always have handy a copy of these regulations
and as many 'old questions' that you can lay your hands upon. It is
obviously essential to have the last five years or so 'old questions' of
your own particular examining board. Then, when you are studying a particular topic, e.g. growth and development, you can wind
up your studies on the subject by glancing at the previous questions
on biology to see roughly what level of knowledge your examiner
requires in that particular topic. You may have time to write
answers to some of these questions as you go along, even when you
are at an early stage in the course. Don't leave the perusal of old
examination papers until the month before the examination. Become familiar with them as soon as you commence your Advanced
Level studies. Incidentally, all students find that the transition from
Ordinary Level studies to Advanced Level studies needs a term or
so for them to make adjustment.

THE COMMENTS OF THE CHIEF EXAMINER

There is one booklet which you may be able to purchase from your
examination board and it will be worth its weight in gold. This
contains the comments of the chief examiner on the previous year's
examinations. (Sometimes, only teachers are permitted to have a
copy.) If possible, obtain two or three editions, because there is a
separate report for each examination year. It is in this booklet that
each subject examiner will make his comments on candidates'
answers to previous questions. Since the examiner must be kept
happy at all costs, it certainly pays handsomely to take time to read
his deliberations on the previous year's examination answers. For

example, one biology examiner complained that in the previous year's answers, candidates had confused the terms 'pathogenic' and 'parthenogenetic'. In addition, he complained that candidates had frequently made imprecise statements about biological matters. They had written, for example, that the 'male and female sex organs are on different flowers' when they should have stated 'on different plants'. You may think that the examiner is fussing but he is the expert and it is he who gives out those vital marks via his assistant-examiners. Every mark counts if you want to obtain those required Advanced Level grades. Try to be precise and accurate in your science studies. This good habit will stand you in good stead, years later, when you are required to make an important clinical decision at a patient's bedside.

3
Methods of studying

Everybody has his or her own preferred method of studying. An old teacher of mine could conceive of no student working properly unless he was seated on a hard chair at a table! Recently, I heard how a successful student could never work unless he was listening to pop music with his eye on the TV – as well as his books. That's remarkable by anybody's standards! Some students can only work in a public library reading room, or similar, in spite of the distractions. Others find it impossible to work unless they have a room to themselves. I must say, I favour a private room that has the air of a study with books, desk or table, and paper and pens etc., all placed together in one spot. Good lighting is essential. The heating of the room should not be too powerful. An atmosphere conducive to sleep is bound to affect concentration and waste hours of valuable time. That brings us to the subject of concentration itself. It is futile trying to study unless we are actually concentrating. The span of concentration in any student will, naturally, vary. Most people can concentrate well for an hour or so, especially if they are reading a subject that they find interesting. After that, energy flags, and so do the powers of concentration. That is the point to relax, briefly, for ten minutes or so. You may care to kick a football around for a short while in the garden, throw a few darts, or play the piano, etc. Beware, however, of resorting in your 'break' to watching television which is likely to take up more than the allotted ten minutes or so. If you become absorbed in the programme – that may be the end of your evening's studies. After a time of relaxation, you will be able to concentrate well for a further period, say

another half to three-quarters of an hour. Then, take another 'break', and so on. There is no point in continuing to read when your concentration finally flags for the evening. Try to begin your evening's study by tackling the more difficult or less interesting subject first. Then, you will be fresh and less likely to lose your powers of concentration. You would do well to leave the study of your favourite subjects to the end of the evening when you are not quite so fresh. By doing this, your natural interest in this subject will help you to keep your mind on the topic in hand. One of the least successful students I can remember would never even allow himself the luxury of a ten minute coffee break during a long stint in the library. Perhaps that does not prove anything, but I doubt if he could concentrate for three to four hours without a break.

Discipline in study is most important. Try to study at the same time, in the same place, each day. Plan out your evenings and afternoons of study and stick to your programme, come what may. Your friends should be told when you are available to see them, and when you are not – because you are working. Try to file your papers neatly, with each subject in its own place. Box files are marvellous for this purpose. Otherwise, you may waste many valuable hours simply looking for lost notes. Of course, it is fair to say that it is not the number of hours that you study, but the quality of your work that counts.

A PARTNER IN CRIME

If you are able, try to find a 'sparring partner', to use a phrase from the world of boxing. What I mean by this is that you find another student who is just as keen and who is taking the same course. If that student knows more than you, so much the better! When I was a medical student, I found the study of anatomy to be difficult, very time-consuming, and complex. Then, I found another student (who subsequently obtained First Class Honours in the subject) and we would give each other regular mini-lectures and questions on anatomy. We would generally debate the subject and look at the corpse, together. I am certain that I passed anatomy partly because of this student's 'improving' effect on my work. In the end, even I could remember the many muscles of the arm and the nerve supply of the hand. It became ingrained in my brain. Take comfort from the fact that memory is supposed to be at its best in the mid- and (especially) late teen-age years. In later life, some of your brain neurones will die every day and leave your memory slightly less efficient.

TEXT-BOOKS

You may have little choice in the text-book which you will use in each subject. Today, there seems to be an abundance of text-books, all professedly aimed at getting you through those important Advanced Level subjects, but your teacher will, no doubt, have his own favourite book and expect you to follow it. Possibly your teacher himself is an author and has actually written all or part of the text-book. Then you will have to use it! You have no choice in the matter. You may, however, at the start of your Advanced Level course, take a dislike to the recommended text-book. Perhaps you hate the type, the format, or the author's way of explaining the various topics. If this is the case, visit a bookshop with a good educational department, and browse through all the text-books in your subjects and at your level of study. Read the preface of each text-book – to see what the author is aiming at. If there is a particular book which covers your course and which appeals to you because of the clear type and diagrams etc., then buy it. It will be a good investment. You are likely to find that this favoured book is your best companion in your long hours of study. Some students find it helpful to underline in red the important topics in the text-book (only cultivate this technique if the book is your own, of course). Then, when you begin to revise, you will be able to quickly refer to the 'bones' of each subject. Please forgive the medical terminology.

CLASS NOTES

Your carefully kept notes made during the lessons of a methodical Advanced Level teacher are very useful and should be read repeatedly. Sometimes a good set of comprehensive notes will almost replace the text-book. (Many students spend hours reading a large text-book but retaining almost nil. This can be a waste of time and effort.)

Unfortunately, some teachers are so disorganized that good note-taking is well-nigh impossible. Ask the previous year's class about the value of their notes taken from each individual teacher's lessons. If these notes were of no use, then you may find that the

'sandwich' scheme (described in the next section) is a useful help
when you are trying to condense your subject to an amount of
knowledge that you can master and remember.

N.B. All class notes should be meticulously stored in clearly-
labelled files. This habit will reap its rewards when you come to
final revision.

CRAM BOOKS AND THE 'SANDWICH' METHOD OF STUDY

That brings us to the important subject of 'cram' books. In recent
years, the large bookshops have sprouted, in abundance, book-
shelves and racks of revision books, all designed to get you through
your Advanced Level examinations in science or art subjects. Some
school teachers are averse to their subject being reduced to a slim
volume. This is understandable, because in the 'slimming' process,
valuable information may be left out. At the end of the day,
however, or to be more exact, in those last desperate days before
your Advanced Level examinations, you will probably be relieved
and confident (if you are an 'average' student) if you have obtained
a firm detailed grasp of the 'cram' book, and nothing else! After all,
most of the authors of these books are experts or examiners and
they are more adept than you at summarizing their subject in a
relatively small number of pages. In this way the subject becomes
manageable, and you acquire an overall view of your studies. Why
not study in 'sandwich' form? When you deal with a new topic, try
starting with the 'cram' book in order to note the basics, and learn
the definitions. Next, read the text-book account of the topic in
order to see it in its context and to obtain more detail. Finally, I
suggest you come back to the 'cram' book to crystallize your
thoughts on that area of your work. At this stage you might be able
to add, neatly in the margin of the 'cram' book, any additional
information which the small book lacks and which you feel your
teacher has indicated that you should know. When I was a clinical
student, I can remember the Professor of Obstetrics remarking,
whilst he stood at a patient's bedside, that he could never understand why it was that students wrongly told examiners that after
delivering the first baby of twins, the obstetrician should wait
twenty minutes or so before delivering the second twin. We knew
the source of information, but didn't dare tell him. It was the small
'aids' book used by most students to help them through the

obstetrics final examination. Naturally, we made certain that it never fell from the pocket of our white coats. The Professor hated such small books on his important subject.

Summary Learn to discipline yourself to study regularly in a suitably quiet environment which is free from distraction. Develop regular habits of study. Don't be led astray by such absorbing distractions as television. Seek out the right books and get on with the work. Every day's study is important because time must not be wasted. On the other hand, take regular respites from your studies, and allot adequate time for physical activity such as sports, etc. In this way you will keep your brain and body in peak condition and dissipate your anxieties. Some students benefit and keep fresh by leaving one day, each week, completely free from study.

4

Mainly about UCCA
and interviews

Every university admissions officer is looking for 'good candidates' to fill his or her course. If the subject is popular, e.g. business studies, law or medicine, then the highest grades can and will be requested, especially at popular universities such as Bristol or Nottingham. So, annually, the dean of each medical school must select a hundred or so new entrants. Naturally, he or she wants the best students who, in turn, want the best medical school place. Firstly, what qualities does the dean seek in new entrants? Secondly, what type of medical school would you, the student, wish to enter?

Qualities sought by the dean

Over the years, because of greatly increased competition for places, almost all medical schools require higher grades for admission than formerly. Once, Advanced Level grades were rarely discussed, but now the dean will request, say, AAA, BBB, or perhaps BBC, when he offers you a provisional place. Unfortunately academic success *seems to have become the main requirement* for many medical schools, some of whom are still prepared to offer a provisional place to a person they have never seen. This is most strange when you consider that the dean may have received a biased report on the candidate's suitability from a well-meaning head teacher, who may never have spoken to the pupil. Much more is needed from a potential doctor than Advanced Level grades. Anyway, until the system is changed, you just have to try and beat it. A professor of mathematics may, understandably, request applicants to his faculty to possess high Advanced Level grades, and little else. On the other hand, a medical school dean should surely take the candidates' other qualities and interests into consideration when he is selecting the doctors of the future. When a retired professor of obstetrics and gynaecology was recently asked which was the most desired attribute in a candidate seeking admission to a medical course, he promptly replied, "Character". Highly-essential qualities in medical students are the ability to communicate verbally and in writing, a willingness to accept responsibility, patience and common-sense, (that immeasurable but important quality – rather like the connective tissue in the mammalian body). Since these qualities are difficult to assess, and such a measurement (and its not impossible to perform) would be time-consuming, medical schools have fallen back on Advanced Level grades as a rough arbitrator of whether or not a student is fit to be a doctor! One wonders just what future patients will make of some of today's students in years to come. *Hundreds* of ideal students (who later obtain good honours degrees or doctorates in other subjects) are turned away every year from a medical school simply because they can't get the right Advanced Level grades (for various good reasons) at the first attempt. You, by the way, should not be amongst these unfortunates after you have read this book thoroughly. Conversely, some totally unsuitable medical students start the expensive course. The Department of Health and Social Security does not seem to want to become involved in the selection process, yet about 9% of those students who pass their final examination never practise medicine. The current selection system has been compared to a maze or a lottery, and, indeed, is one for the uninitiated applicant.

Your choice of medical school

Which type of medical school would you like to enter? Again, unless you are brilliant, you cannot afford to be fussy! A place at any British medical school is like gold, nowadays. Nevertheless, *if you feel certain* that you will obtain three grade Bs at Advanced Level, then you can be choosey and should ask yourself the following questions:

• Does the course, as described in the university prospectus, seem to have the right emphasis? For example, if you have thoughts of becoming a GP – does the medical school have a professor of general practice and a proper course of instruction in primary health care at a suitable health centre? (Most medical school teaching is still based on selected patients in a hospital environment, even though about 60% of students will become general practitioners and not hospital specialists.) On the other hand, perhaps you like the idea of entering medical research. You would be wise to think of a medical school such as Manchester with its good facilities for post-graduate work.

• Are there adequate junior hospital jobs for you when you qualify? For example, Bristol and Cardiff feed the large number of hospitals in their region with junior doctors who are doing their first year's jobs. This is important to bear in mind with the present surplus of newly-qualified doctors. Nowadays, Cardiff attempts to guarantee that its newly-qualified doctors will be able to obtain twelve months' work in the hospitals of Wales.

• Is the medical school handy to cheap (student) accommodation? This is an important consideration. The medical course is long and expensive, in spite of a university grant, and books and instruments are costly.

THE UCCA (APPLICATION) FORM

This is a particularly important section. Unfortunately, your chances of entering a medical school may hinge on the very manner in which you complete your UCCA form. It is on this form that you must declare your choice of the five medical schools which you would most like to attend. Some years ago, you could apply to, and be accepted by, half a dozen medical schools. Then, after the Advanced Level results, you would accept the place that you fancied most! Birmingham Medical School used to try and avoid being let down by candidates when they asked for a £5.00 or so, deposit from you when they offered a provisional place. Those days are gone, the dean is now in the driving seat.

Medical school applications are now handled by the Universities' Central Council on Admissions (UCCA). Oxford and Cambridge still have their own entrance procedures. It is worth remembering that if you can pass the Oxford entrance examination and interview, you may be offered a provisional place on the strength of this provided that you can obtain, in addition, three very modest

Advanced Level passes, for example, DDD. Think carefully before applying to Cambridge, unless you are brilliant, since AAA grades are normally needed.

COMPLETING YOUR UCCA FORM

Applications should reach UCCA between 1 September and 15 December of the year prior to the year when you wish to commence at medical school. The closing date if you are applying to Oxford or Cambridge is 15 October.

• When you complete the UCCA form, remember that the very order in which you name your choice of medical school may have a significant influence on whether you will obtain a provisional offer and one day become a doctor. Your handwriting should be easily legible and neat. *Return your UCCA form promptly.* If you delay until November or December, your chance of an offer may be reduced.

   First, find out which Advanced Level grades are currently required by all the medical schools. For example, the Middlesex Medical School has been recently requesting a minimum of BBC grades for successful applicants, whereas the University of Wales College of Medicine currently requires BBB. (People do get places with less than these grades sometimes.) Again, Manchester might ask for BBC at your first attempt, but AAA if you fail first time and want another shot. Edinburgh won't normally give you a second chance at all, neither does Dundee. This is worth bearing in mind when you fill in the UCCA form.

• You will find that Appendix 1 and 2 contain much useful information about the various medical schools.

• Here is another important point to remember. When completing the UCCA form, remember that unless you put certain medical schools in a high place of choice (usually first) those medical schools probably won't want to know you. Medical schools with this independent reputation include Bristol, Nottingham, Southampton and Glasgow. Alternatively, the University of Wales College of Medicine will still consider you, even if you list them as your fourth or fifth choice. This is well worth remembering. (Don't waste your first choice with the University of Wales College of Medicine, therefore.) Oxford, also, is not fussy about its position on the UCCA form, but do not mention Cambridge!

You are advised to write to various medical schools and enquire about their requested entrance grades and any preferred order which they request on the UCCA form. Deans are now much more forthcoming than formerly.

- Another important fact is this. Remember that a provisional offer from a medical school that requires 'only' BCC is very well worth having (if you can get it) since, statistically, you are more likely to obtain BCC than BBB. Common-sense, isn't it? Unfortunately, though, as was explained in an earlier chapter, these medical schools make fewer offers in proportion to each actual place to be filled. Your sixth form teachers will normally give you your prospects at Advanced Level, after a couple of terms with them. Incidentally, your estimated grades are sent to UCCA. Apply for those medical schools whose examination requirements you seem likely to meet in due course. A book which is well worth consulting is *Degree Course Offers* by Brian Heap (careers consultant). This book would be handy, also, if you unfortunately fail to enter medical school but you wanted details of other university courses. It contains much useful information on the attitudes which deans and admissions officers (at various universities) hold towards their applicants.

- Don't forget to add your hobbies, interests and school activities to the appropriate section of the UCCA form. An unusual hobby may catch the eye of a bored dean sifting through hundreds of application forms. This small section on the application form gives you, in effect, the opportunity to advertise yourself, but write these sentences after much thought.

Summary Do consider applying to those medical schools with the *lowest requirements*, but remember that here, your outside interests declared on the UCCA form and your performance at interview will have more influence on whether you are offered a provisional place. If you do receive the provisional offer of a 'BCC place', then, of course, you stand a better chance of being able to get these grades and hence of taking up the offer.

INTERVIEWS FOR A PLACE AT MEDICAL SCHOOL

Usually, the medical school want to see you in person before they make a provisional offer. Always be punctual in attendance for an

interview. This may require an over-night stay in the town so that you can be certain of being at the interview on time. Firstly, check that your appearance befits that of a future doctor. This is most important when you are seeking to create a good first time impression in a space of only ten or fifteen minutes. Although there are 'punk' students studying at medical schools, this is not the norm and it is difficult to see how they obtained a place. Either there was no interview before they were accepted, or they went 'punk' to celebrate passing the examinations. Perhaps you have other theories. Nottingham, by the way, never gives a provisional offer without interviewing the candidate. Leicester and most London schools also place great value on the interview. If interviews are not your strong point or you are prone to 'stage nerves', then consider applying to a university such as Dundee or Leeds where they are less likely to want to see you before making you a provisional offer.

In deciding what to wear at interview, men would be advised to choose a two-piece suit and dark tie. You are seeking a place to train in what is a traditional and conservative profession. Second choice is a smart sports jacket and trousers. Denim trousers are not advisable, though I do know of a senior consultant who wears a denim suit. Did he wear the same clothes at his interview prior to consultant appointment? I doubt it. For women a suit or dress would be ideal – trousers should perhaps be avoided. The emphasis should be on a neat and tidy appearance, and ostentation should be avoided.

Interviews vary in length and content. Fifteen minutes is about average and there will be usually two or three persons interviewing you. Remember that these persons are successful members of their profession and naturally feel that the way they have accomplished things is the only way to success. (You may have other views but do not voice them.) Some of your interviewers will not be qualified in medicine. They will have trained in biochemistry, microbiology, or a similar discipline.

Hints for appearing at interview

- Don't appear over-confident, and try not to turn your back on the interviewers whilst you are entering the room and closing the door. Look the questioners straight in the eye. Try to avoid answering a question by merely responding 'Yes' or 'No.'

Qualify your reply – your interviewers want to sit back, listen to you, and not make all the running. They may be bored by all interviews and interviewees, but attend to oblige the dean.

● Try to find out (from the medical school's prospectus) as much as possible about the course before the interview, but don't be afraid to make any enquiries concerning the course or the medical school itself, if you are given the chance to ask questions. When given the opportunity, try to ask intelligent, well-informed questions which will favourably influence your interview committee. Enquire, for example, about their major fields of research. That should get some of the interviewers roused.

● Before the interview, attempt to find out more about the dean and his interests from a 'Medical Directory' or, if he is in there, and important enough, 'Who's Who?'. These books are to be found in reference libraries. If you should be interviewed by the dean himself and have the same interests or hobbies and can gently engineer the interview into this direction, you are very fortunate indeed. This needs great tact, however, but could guarantee you that provisional offer in the face of strong competition.

● Be prepared to talk about any hobbies or activities you have named on your UCCA form. This means that you don't boast about accomplishments which you do not possess.

● Remember your interviewers are mainly hospital specialists and these may not feel too enthusiastic about your stressing that you want to enter general practice of which subject they probably have limited knowledge. Unfortunately, very few interviewers are general practitioners, who could add balance to the interview board. If you are asked which branch of medicine you want to enter, do not be afraid to reply that you are undecided in the matter. That is a perfectly reasonable response on your part. After all, your own view of medicine is still very limited. Deans must become tired of hearing would-be entrants saying that they would like to be neuro-surgeons, plastic surgeons, or such like.

● The question 'Why do *you* want to study medicine?' is almost a certainty. Be especially prepared to give your own frank and honest reply to this question, and especially avoid the hackneyed phrase, 'I want to help people'. Why not express an interest in anaesthetics or some other subject which appeals to you?

- Should there be an open day at the medical school prior to your interview, you would be wise to attend, especially if this medical school is your first choice on the UCCA form. You could write to the dean and enquire about this facility. Later, at interview, you could discuss what you saw in the various departments.

- Try to read a quality daily newspaper in order to create an awareness of current affairs. Especially read items with a medical content.

- Do not hint that your parents have influenced you in your choice of career. Above all, show undivided and strong personal commitment to medicine. Your interviewers will find this hard to resist.

- Try to have some knowledge of, and interest in, the health problems of your own home town/area. One applicant for a place at a London medical school had three 'A' grades and one 'B' grade − an impressive array of results. However, he was not offered a place because he showed no interest in the health problems of his own locality which suffered a high rate of unemployment.

- Remember that you will create 75% of your over-all impression on the dean and his assistants in the first thirty seconds of your interview.

- *One final tip about preparing to be interviewed.* Ask somebody (e.g. a teacher, lecturer, doctor or business-man) to stage a mock interview for you. This could be an excellent preparation for your medical school interview, and is a good place to 'drop any clangers'.

N.B. If you have good Ordinary Level (and possibly Advanced Level) passes but are unable to obtain an interview anywhere, then your school report may be the reason. I can only suggest that you discuss this problem with your head teacher and careers officer.

OVERSEAS APPLICANTS TO MEDICAL SCHOOL

Overseas students now have increasing difficulty in finding a medical school place in the United Kingdom and also in obtaining the necessary financial support required for the five or six years spent as an undergraduate. Not only is there keen competition for places from British applicants, but most medical schools are limited in the number of overseas students whom they can admit. For example, King's College School of Medicine, London, can only admit two overseas students each Autumn. This quota has been established by the Department of Health and Social Security through the University of London.

Those fortunate overseas students who are accepted will need to provide, to the University, a financial guarantee that they can maintain themselves and pay the necessary tuition fees during the degree course. It should be remembered that it may cost £4000 annually to live and study in, for example, London. In addition, medical school fees could be £9000 per annum for clinical students. It should be noted that grants for overseas students, from either the candidate's own government or the British Council, can be very difficult to obtain. (You may be able to obtain further details from the corresponding embassy, consulate-general or students' office in London.)

Overseas applicants should apply in the usual way through UCCA. The address is the General Secretary, UCCA, PO Box 28, Cheltenham, Glos, GL50 1HY. The closing date for applications is 15 December of the year prior to the year in which the course commences. Applications should reach UCCA by 15 October if one of the choices includes Oxford or Cambridge. Overseas applicants who want details of exemption from O and A level passes should write to the appropriate University. If you are applying to the University of London, exemption details can be obtained from the Senate House, Malet Street, London, WC1E 7HU.

5
The Advanced Level examinations on the horizon

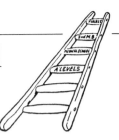

In theory, your Advanced Level studies should widen your knowledge of the three subjects that you are studying, and this information will then form a foundation for you when you eventually arrive at university. In practice, most of what you learn at Advanced Level will be quickly forgotten. Years later, when you are a qualified doctor and see patients, you will muse over the relevance of Advanced Level studies to your life's work – especially when you are trying to manage a patient whose problems are mainly social or mental. Then, you will wish you had studied psychology or sociology at Advanced Level, rather than physics or chemistry!

It is most regrettable that those who want to become medical students are forced to specialize in science subjects so early in their academic studies. It will be much later in life that medical practitioners (like many other scientists) will realize that early specialization has reduced their familiarity with history, literature and music, etc. A knowledge of these subjects could only make a better medical practitioner out of the student.

In fact, Advanced Level examinations are probably the most difficult that you will sit. The curriculum in each subject at Advanced Level is usually wide, especially in the ever-expanding science subjects. The course will probably be covered at a brisk canter by your teachers, and your chief examiners are probably university lecturers who might well be somewhat out of touch with life in the sixth form, especially since they will possibly have never taught in a school. A recent Advanced Level maths paper evoked many complaints from school teachers, and a university professor compared the questions to those set at degree examinations. On the other hand, later, when you sit your university examinations, you will at least know that your teachers help to both set and mark your answers.

It should be stressed that your first attempt at Advanced Levels may be your only chance to enter the medical profession. Some medical schools don't like 'second time round' students at all, and most deans would ask you to obtain even higher grades at your second attempt. Besides all this, a failure at your first attempt may be so depressing that you could not face another try the following year. You will need, therefore, to be at your peak performance on the first occasion that you take Advanced Level examinations. Six months at least before your first examination therefore, start to plan out your revision, even though you are still treading on fresh ground in the course during the day. Put aside a few hours each week for answering old examination questions and for looking through topics you have studied before, especially in those areas of the syllabus that you do not fully understand. Never be afraid to ask your teacher/tutor to run through any difficult topics, at their convenience. Large Advanced Level classes mean that individual instruction is unlikely, but at least you can pester your mentors to explain, once again, a subject which you do not fully understand. Alternatively, get hold of a different text book and study that difficult topic as it is explained by a different author. This new book may throw a fresh light on the matter. Then, summarize the topic and write it into the margin of your own text-book or cram book. Above all, plan your revision programme in good time for the examination. It is better to revise the whole course briefly than to miss out large chunks by spending too long reading a few topics.

CRAM COURSES AND PERSONAL TUTORS

During the Christmas holiday and especially the Easter holiday, before your Advanced Levels, you may find it difficult to maintain the momentum of your personal studies. In addition, you may have now discovered that you are weak in one or other of the three subjects which you are taking. The answer to these problems may be a 'holiday revision course,' details of which are usually advertised in the educational columns of the quality newspapers. They are especially designed for pupils in the second year of the sixth form. Because you will probably need to pay for food and lodging whilst you attend the course, a substantial financial element may be involved. It may be worth it, however. Make quite sure, before you attend such a course, that it will be a preparation for your particular examination board's papers and also that the tutors are completely familiar with Advanced Level examination technique. Your week's residential tutorial could well improve your ultimate Advanced Level grades, especially if you would have been wasting that week at home. A change of scene will relax you, too. Many Easter revision courses will give you a 'mock' examination at the end of the week's course and this will provide you with a provisional estimate of your grade in the forthcoming summer Advanced Level examinations. This may well give you a boost of confidence – or, alternatively, show up some of your weak spots. The whole emphasis of the vacational revision course should be on tuition and discussion in a small group.

The parents of many Advanced Level pupils seek out a regular personal tutor for their offspring, usually at a cost of anything from £5–10 per hour. The bright candidate won't need such help, but for the average pupil it might make all the difference between success and failure, especially in a weak subject. The tutor must be well-versed in preparing students for Advanced Level examinations and, hopefully, may even mark papers for one of the Advanced Level boards. Such tutors are not easy to find and you may well need the personal recommendation of a candidate who was success-ful with his Advanced Level examinations a year or two before you come to take them. A good tutor, who meets you for help and discussion for an hour or two each week, could make a significant improvement to your final grades. The more you discuss your subjects, the more likely you are to retain, in your memory, the basic and important facts of that subject. (That is why a 'sparring' partner is so useful as described in Chapter 2.)

MENTAL AND PHYSICAL FITNESS

Try to prevent yourself from the staleness caused by excessive hours spent at the books and not enough time spent in relaxation. Start a regular form of exercise that is not too demanding in terms of time. Badminton and swimming are two examples. These sports can be fitted easily into your schedule of studies in a series of regular 'doses'. You can also take an additional spell at these exercises when you are fed up with the books and work is depressing you.

Afterwards, even though you are physically tired, you may still have enough mental energy to spend time on an essay or reading a couple of chapters.

YOUR VISION

Your eyesight is very important, naturally. If you have any doubts at all as to whether you need glasses for looking at the blackboard or text-books, then pay a visit to the local optician who will test your eyes and tell you if you need glasses. There is no charge for an eye test.

HAY FEVER

This may be the point to mention that curse of many students – hay-fever. The maximum incidence of this sometimes disabling condition coincides exactly with the peak of Advanced Level examination activity. The cause of hay-fever is the grass pollen grain which is highly irritating to the mucous membranes of the nose and the conjunctivae of certain susceptible individuals. In fact, about 20% of young persons suffer to some degree, and it is obvious that in many instances their examination performance is adversely affected. Make a friend of your GP and go along and chat to him at a time when he is not too busy (avoid Mondays and Fridays)! Tell him you are afraid that your hay-fever will affect your studies and examination results. Ask him for a remedy that will *not* make you drowsy and unable to concentrate on your final revision and later when you actually come to writing your examination papers. You are certain to have your GP's sympathy, especially when he or she realises that you have set your heart on a career in medicine.

PSYCHOSOMATIC ILLNESS

You may also need medical advice if you suffer from psychosomatic conditions such as asthma or eczema, because these illnesses are aggravated by the stress involved in preparing for those vital Advanced Level examinations. Bad asthma attacks are largely preventable by modern drugs and inhalers. Consult your general practitioner about this in good time before your examinations.

SPECIAL HEALTH PROBLEMS OF FEMALE STUDENTS

The examination performance of many female students may be adversely affected by their monthly periods, especially if they are sitting an important examination just prior to or during a heavy or painful menstrual period. Provided that the student consults her general practitioner a month or so in advance, it should be possible to adjust the timing and extent of menstruation. It is quite justifiable to take the appropriate hormone treatment for such an occasion as the most significant examination that you will ever take.

REGULAR REVISION

In the last six months before Advanced Levels, use some of your study time to periodically revise what you have covered already. This makes the 'big' final revision so much more palatable. You may be able to acquire the useful habit of reading more rapidly than you do already. (There are various books to help you achieve this skill.) If, for example, you are revising an easy page of a text-book, you should be able to read at a rate of almost 600 words per minute, with practice. If the page is more detailed, you need to be able to read at about a quarter to a third of this rate, i.e. about 150–200 words per minute. The ability to read rapidly is a most useful tool for the Advanced Level candidate and potential medical student. It will enable you to revise more topics in those last few days or weeks before the actual examination, and this information will then be more easily recalled.

WHAT TO DO WHEN YOU ARE DEPRESSED AND THINK YOU WILL FAIL

From time to time during their course, *all* students think that they can't possibly pass their forthcoming Advanced Level examinations. I remember on at least one occasion that I threw my physics text-books around the room in desperation – a good safety valve providing nothing is damaged. Firstly you may become depressed about your studies generally and feel that you are absorbing nothing. Then, as a result, you become anxious about the time being wasted. This is a perfectly normal reaction and usually means that you need a short break from your studies, after which you will

be able to stand back and assess your objectives. Maths, for example, may seem irrelevant to medicine, but in a year or two you will be standing in a hospital ward, listening to an expert showing you how to recognise an interesting disease in a real live patient. Doesn't that spur you on? Your Advanced Level course is a short but necessary phase in your studies. Further, just think of those very ordinary students who passed their grades last year. Doesn't that encourage you? After a few days of such philosophic deliberations, interest in your subjects will always revive, especially if you have had a short break reading a novel, or taking some physical exercise or other form of light relief. Few students can study without any break. I like that saying of the old Greek scholar, Euripides, 'Enough sufficeth for the wise'.

6

More about examinations, including the day itself

Unfortunately, medical school entrance and success with Advanced Level examinations are fast becoming synonymous. One medical school dean recently commented, 'Far more applicants could cope academically with the course in medicine than can be accepted'. Careers officers are now consulted by bright pupils who have discovered that they have an excellent chance of obtaining high grades in their future Advanced Level examinations. Simply because of this, these sixth formers now believe that they should direct their energies towards entering medical school, rather than 'wasting' their high grades. To desire to embark upon a lifetime in medicine simply because you are in the top echelons of examination performers is surely undesirable. Compassion, a liking for one's fellow human beings, an appetite for long working hours, and the ability to accept responsibility are far more desirable qualities in a potential doctor than success in examinations with little sympathy for the patient and no genuine interest in medicine. Fortunately, some enlightened (but too few) medical school deans are now beginning to reject those candidates who have examination ability but little else. Good for them!

Medical practitioners have always suffered an above-average incidence of suicide. It may be that this incidence will rise further in the long term future when frustrated doctors, who find it difficult to relate to people, are unable, because of competition, to find a job where they don't need to handle patients and their problems. In the past, it has not been too difficult for young doctors to specialize in a subject where there is low patient contact, e.g laboratory work such as pathology. (In passing, it is interesting to note that for years, because of extreme competition for places, Australian medical schools have been known to admit only those in the very top range of intelligence.)

This book is intended for hard-working students who know that they possess the right qualities to practise medicine, but who realize also, that they may not obtain a place in medical school, because they could have difficulty in getting high examination grades.

Incidentally, some medical schools will be impressed by any relevant medical 'experience' that you have gained from hospital, laboratory or similar work during your school holidays. This is not essential, however.

THE FINAL REVISION

Successful candidates are usually those who work steadily over a two year period and who aim to arrive at their peak performance during the Advanced Level month – normally June. It is frustrating that the greatest mental effort is expected of a student when summer begins to show its face.

If you have revised steadily and practised old questions continually, there is no need at all to panic in the last few weeks before the examinations. Continue to allow a short time for physical activity or sport in order to reduce your level of anxiety. Memory performance drops when anxiety levels rise. At all costs *you must avoid a state of panic* when you may be totally unable to recall even the rudiments of your subject and your confidence drops to zero as failure looms large on the horizon. (General practitioners often see such unfortunate cases during the examination period.) It is an avoidable state of affairs in the vast majority of students. A *few* anxious candidates may benefit from a short course of tranquillizers just before and during the examinations. This is quite acceptable provided no drowsiness is incurred and the tablets are used for a short period only. Then, there is no likelihood of addiction or dependence. After all, this may be the only time in your whole life that you need to take such medication. You should consult your family doctor about this.

WHEN THE PACE QUICKENS . . .

In the final two weeks, you will be finding that your 'cram' book
and personal notes are worth their weight in gold, especially since
lack of time will prevent you from reading long chapters of your
text-books. Try writing out the essentials of each main topic on
small filing cards and also give yourself a mock examination from
old examination questions which you have never seen before. This
latter activity will help you to time your performance in the
imminent examination.

At this final stage, also, it may be worth your while looking at a
book of old questions containing model *answers* and written by an
expert. This will remind you of the manner in which your examination answers should be set out and answered. If you have worked
steadily, you will now be encouraged by what you know and can
write and will be ready for the battle with the examiner.

THE ADVANCED LEVEL EXAMINATION

General examination hints

You should never start writing as soon as you have seen the
question paper. Beat the examiner is the name of the game.
Therefore, spend five to ten minutes reading through the paper and
inspecting it generally before you lift your pen. It's hard to believe
that these questions were concocted at least eighteen months
previously. If there is a choice, decide very carefully which questions will suit you best. One wrong selection here could cost you a
grade and a place in medical school. Start by answering your *best*
question in order to gain confidence, but don't exceed the time
allowed for answering that part of the paper. *You must tackle all
the required questions.* It is relatively easy to obtain the first ten
marks in a twenty mark question, but very difficult to exceed
seventeen marks out of twenty in such a question. Try to decide
what degree of detail is required in your answering of each
question. For example, if the question asks you to name five
processes, then there is no need to describe them in detail. Be clear
on the meaning of such words as: compare, describe, explain,
outline, enumerate, distinguish and contrast. Look them up in the
dictionary if necessary. All these words form the lingo of the
examiner who has set your questions. Try not to include irrelevant

details in your answers. This will waste your valuable time, and you will not score any further marks. *Your written answers must be legible and neat.* Remember that your examiner is marking hundreds of papers and your tidiness is bound to impress him – to your advantage. It is unwise to rely on 'spotting' examination questions since you will be instantly demoralized when you first look at the examination paper and see the absence of your favoured topics. In any case, examiners try to set questions as widely as possible within the syllabus. Sometimes they even exceed their brief and ask questions on topics you do not need to know. When this happens, your teachers generally send a volley of complaints to the chief examiner.

Once the Advanced Level examinations have started, you will need to spend some hours relaxing between the various question papers. Don't try to work all day and every day between examinations or you will quickly become stale and your performance will decline.

Examination hints for three advanced level subjects

Here are some hints contributed by teachers in the main Advanced Level subjects.

Physics

With the examination a day or two ahead, make sure that you have thoroughly revised those topics with which you are most familiar. It is now too late to start learning those subjects which you never properly grasped, anyway. It will be essential to have memorized the main laws, definitions and equations.

A good many valuable marks are lost by candidates who write unexplained statements on their answer papers. When answering problems, especially numerical questions, always explain on your paper, to the examiner, just how it is that you have arrived at the answer you have written down. The making of these written explanations will also help you to think things through as you write the paper. You can also lose marks simply because you fail to add the necessary units to your final numerical answers.

Marks will be lost by sloppy diagrams which are squashed and inadequately labelled. Don't be afraid to include a small explanatory diagram if your answer merits this, even if your examiner has not specifically requested it. Such a diagram will help you to work through the problem, and indeed is essential in the mechanics questions when forces are involved.

As far as the physics practical examination is concerned, it will be necessary to be certain that you are thoroughly familiar with all the various pieces of apparatus and that you know how to handle them. During the examination, marks will be gained if you make as many readings as time permits, and then calculate the 'mean' reading for your final result.

Biology

The essay questions should be made your priority, because they score heavily in marks at almost all examination boards. Before you commence your essay, make rough notes to plan out what you are going to write. Then, number these rough notes in the order in which you plan to write them into your essay answer. The examiner will take notice of a planned essay with *adequate sub-headings*.

Don't spend a disproportionate time on the short questions and 'pass' any that you can't immediately answer, otherwise you will be held up wasting valuable time. Come back to any short questions you have missed when you have finished all the other parts of the question paper.

Practical examination in biology

You would be wise to follow closely the instructions that you are given from the examination sheet. Do your practical work in the order suggested and dissect only those structures which you have been requested to display. Don't mis-spell any word which the examiner has already given you on the question sheet. Mistakes such as this will not create much of an impression and you may well lose marks anyway. It will be a great advantage if you can practise dissecting additional rats (or whatever animal is set) in your own time at home. Dissecting ability improves enormously with practice.

In the practical examination, you should immediately write down any readings that you may make. Otherwise, they will probably be forgotten in the excitement and tension of the practical test. Always label your test-tubes in any experiments.

N.B. A useful study book for biology, and which some schools cannot now afford because of financial cuts, is *Biology – A Functional Approach*, published by Nelson. It has a companion book called *The Biology Study Guide*. Both books have an attractive layout and would be an excellent investment if your school does not supply them already. Who knows, your purchasing these books could make all the difference as to whether or not you pursue a career in medical school!

Chemistry

In the weeks before the Advanced Level examinations, you should check that you understand the basic concepts of the course. Valuable marks will be lost if you give imprecise definitions. Revise the essential chemical formulae very carefully, and make certain of the units of measurement.

Continue to try 'old' questions from not only your own examination board but also from any other board which sets a similar style of question. Thereby, you will gain confidence to have a bash at the unfamiliar question which your Advanced Level examiner may pose.

Organic synthetic methods may be easier to memorize if maps of organic reactions are sketched during your revision. These maps will remind you of the major routes between the different classes of organic compounds.

The following two (companion) books will help you to revise for Advanced Level chemistry. They will be especially useful from Easter until you take the Advanced Level examinations in June. Both of these books are published by Arnold: *Questions and Solutions for A Level Chemistry* by Peter Brown (Book 1 – Questions, Book 2 – Solutions). Book 2 is especially useful since it contains model answers, mark schemes and comments.

The practical examination
Some examination boards have now dispensed with the practical examination in favour of continual assessment during your sixth form years. The following hints may help you where the examination board still holds the time-honoured three hour practical examination.

- First, read the whole paper and decide how much time you should allot to each item of work (i.e. just as you did in the

written papers.) Some examination boards actually give guidance
on the practical paper concerning the allotment of your time.

• Try to decide if the examiner is looking primarily for accuracy of
calculation or for the quality of your observation. If it is the
latter, then do not waste valuable minutes struggling with small
calculations which count for very few marks.

• Normally, you are allowed to take reference books into the
Chemistry practical examination. You will find it much more
convenient to consult a small and specially written 'bench' book,
rather than having to hunt through a large text-book.

7
All may not be lost

It is hoped that you will not need to study the contents of this chapter. But it is wise to consider the possibilities that exist if you should fail to obtain your Advanced Level grades at the first attempt. Remember that it is probably easier to obtain a provisional offer for medical school entrance, than it is to actually obtain the requested examination results. You will notice from Table 2 in Appendix 1 that whereas Manchester is prepared to make 600 conditional offers, only 200 persons will achieve the required grades and opt to go there. If your provisional offers (and you are able to accept two) depend on your obtaining BBB grades, i.e. twelve points (A = 5, B = 4, C = 3, D = 2, E = 1) then it is unlikely that you will be able to take up your place if you obtain only BBC grades, i.e. eleven points.

Can anything be done if you just miss your required grades? (It is obvious that you should plan to be at home, and not, for example, travelling the continent when your results are published.) It is advisable to immediately contact the dean's office, by telephone or first class letter, stating your results and pointing out that you are still available and keen to start. You may still be fortunate. Much will depend on national Advanced Level pass rates. Some years produce more pupils with high grades than others. At one London medical school, about two years ago, because of high pass rates, there were insufficient places for those who *had* obtained the required grades. Confusion reigned for a while. Some students agreed to postpone their entry to medical school for twelve months – to the dean's great relief, I imagine!

If you have failed to obtain admission by only one point, then you could be fortunate to obtain a place through the UCCA 'clearing' system during September, or even October. Believe it or not, some successful students who have obtained a place will have second thoughts about studying medicine and decide to start an engineering or other unrelated course. This could be your opportunity if you apply through the UCCA clearing system.

TAKING STOCK OF THE SITUATION IF YOU HAVE FAILED TO OBTAIN A PLACE

- You could decide to have another attempt at your Advanced Levels. At first, this will be a bitter pill to swallow, but if you are keen, it is worthwhile, and repeating your studies will doubtless become more palatable as the next year passes. Another year's study could make all the difference to your grades provided that you use your time profitably. Advanced Level examinations do not seem such an extraordinary hurdle and are usually less fearsome, when you tackle them for a second time. One difficulty, though, is that you must re-apply again through UCCA, and your medical school may not be too impressed with second-timers. If you are uncertain about the position, write yourself (not your parents) to the dean of that medical school and ask him what is his attitude to pupils who are re-sitting Advanced Levels. Some deans will admire your enthusiasm, especially if they have failed an examination themselves.

  Try to analyse why you failed. Was it insufficient study, poor teaching, large classes, poor examination technique, ill-health on the 'big day', or just the wrong questions? Would it be better if you left school and went to a technical college for the next year before a second attempt at your Advanced Levels? Many technical college principals claim that their Advanced Level results are superior to those of the local schools. Perhaps you could afford to spend twelve months at a good 'cramming' college which produces results if little else.

- If your examination results are good enough for another university course (but not high enough to start to study medicine) then you might decide to study for an honours degree in one of the science subjects. This could, in time, lead you to entering medical school as a post-graduate. Some medical schools will consider taking good honours graduates. Try Bristol, Southampton, or Sheffield. An honours degree in physiology, biochemistry or microbiology might carry some weight if you are applying as a mature student. (I do know of one graduate engineer who is currently studying medicine.) It is most important to remember that if you are a *graduate* entering medical school, then you may find it difficult to obtain a grant from your local authority — especially for the first 2–3 years of your course. It is worth noting that entry to medical school via an honours degree is *not* easy. About one in twenty (only) of all medical school entrants will be honours graduates.

• You may decide, having failed your grades, that you do not wish to proceed further with your attempt to enter medical school. This is quite understandable. Don't be despondent, you are in good company and still among the brightest of your contemporaries. Have you considered accountancy or a course in management? What about the four year course in osteopathy at the London School of Osteopathy? (Fringe medicine will boom in the next decade as more and more research is carried out into the adverse reactions of many drugs.) At this point, you could seek the advice of a careers officer/teacher.

Dentistry and optics, old stand-by's of those who fail to enter medical school, are less likely to welcome you since they have plenty of applicants who have placed those professions as their first choice. You might just be able to get into pharmacy, especially if you are willing to consider a place at a polytechnic. If you have failed to obtain the necessary grades but have reasonable results, it is well worth sitting down by the 'phone and ringing around various universities immediately, to see what vacancies they have in their various courses.

• This is a real shot in the dark. If you have a kind relative who would sponsor you, would you consider studying medicine abroad in a university whose degrees are recognized here, for example, India? If you are really keen, and you have the finance, it might be worth looking into this. You could then return after you have qualified, to continue your work in this country. After all, five or six years abroad isn't long when you consider that you will be practising medicine for forty years.

• Here is a last suggestion if you fail to find a place in any medical school but have reasonable grades. Try telephoning around the deans' offices about 4–5 days after the October term has commenced. By this time, some new students will have already dropped out from the course. Perhaps, because of psychological reasons, they could not face up to the dissection of the cadaver. By this time also, those students on the medical school's reserve list may have applied for other courses. Your telephone call (or letter) could now prove timely and produce a place for you.

8
Congratulations! You have made it to medical school

This chapter is written to serve two purposes. Firstly, it is meant to be read while you are studying for Advanced Levels, so that you may be inspired to press on towards what you most desire to do – see and examine and treat real patients. Secondly, here are some further details concerning the five year course which you have been so keen to commence. It is amazing how many students attend for a medical school interview and yet know very little of the actual course.

It is now assumed that you have achieved your required grades, taken up your provisional offer and are about to start at medical school. Congratulations! The transition from school to medical school is dramatic, to say the least. You will enjoy it immensely. It is the job of the dean and his staff to mould a motley crowd of raw students into newly-qualified young doctors who earn money and take responsibility for the lives of patients. There are only five years to complete this training procedure and the medical course becomes more crowded every year. For the dean and his staff, this task is almost as great as that of selecting the new entrants for medical school. The dean must watch, with great trepidation, when his former students, now armed with brand new medical degrees, leave medical school for the last time. Fortunately, the vast majority of young doctors know their limitations only too well and there are plenty of seniors to consult during the first few years after qualification. Once a student, always a student . . .

THE PRE-CLINICAL CURRICULUM

The first part of the medical course is concerned with studying the basic sciences and you will be learning the physiology, anatomy and biochemistry of the human body. A variable amount of time is spent dissecting the human body and you will very quickly become used to violating the human form. All this work will fascinate you. Useful qualities to possess are the ability to select and learn the fundamentals of these pre-clinical subjects, and a good memory. As for your university teachers, some will be poor at imparting information, while others will be gifted academics who have an infectious enthusiasm for their subject. Many of your teachers, at this stage of the course, are not, themselves, medically qualified. But all naturally believe that their own subject is the main content of the medical course, and they infer that everything else you learn is of lesser importance. During this period, you will be preparing for the day when you first enter the hospital wards and clinics. It will arrive much sooner than you imagine.

The pre-clinical part of the curriculum is normally of five terms' duration and is terminated by the second MB examination which is rated to be 'stiff'. There is one advantage for you as a university student. This is that your teachers will examine you, unlike Advanced Level examinations. (In some medical schools, considerable emphasis is placed on a continual assessment of the student rather than on one second MB examination at the end of the five terms.) It's true that there will also be an external examiner (from another university) present at your second MB examinations but he is likely to agree with your own teachers' assessment of your ability. If you have obtained your grades at Advanced Level, there is no reason why you will not, with steady work, which is now your ingrained habit, obtain your second MB examination quite comfortably at the first attempt. Such is the rejoicing by medical students when they pass second MB, that onlookers would be forgiven for thinking that they had already qualified as doctors. In actual fact, there are still three important years to follow. Nevertheless, the passing of second MB means that a great hurdle has been passed.

THE CLINICAL PART OF THE COURSE

The last three years of the course will be spent mainly in the wards of the teaching and other hospitals, the operating theatres, the

out-patient clinics, and to a lesser extent, in the hospital laborator-
ies and X-ray rooms. Even the mortuary will become a familiar
place! Naturally, lectures continue in the usual fashion – the good,
bad and mediocre. Unfortunately, when Professors and clinical
teachers are appointed, there is little or no assessment made of their
ability to impart information to the student. One wonders whether
the interview committee appointing a consultant or clinical teacher
has ever heard that person give a lecture. Good teachers will make a
lasting impression on you, and their words of advice will echo
down the years when you later examine a difficult case. I well
remember one professor who used to frequently throw out the
statement 'Don't forget that there is no such thing as psychogenic
pus'. That is worth remembering when you are called to see a
patient with a fever which normally has an organic cause, although
this may not be obvious at your first examination.

All the time, during these three exciting years, you will be
learning how to talk to the patients (i.e. obtain a history) and how
to examine him or her. Quite early on in your days as a clinical
student, you will be called 'doctor' by the patient for the first time.
You will find this extremely strange but also very encouraging. If
you are honest, you will stop to explain to the patient that you are
still a student but, sometimes, you will overlook this! Taking a
patient's history and conducting a physical examination requires a
considerable amount of practice and skill, but you will improve
with experience. There are many pit-falls, nevertheless. Self-
confidence and the ability to communicate, together with a knowledge of how people live, will prove great assets to you. All this time
you will be learning about fascinating disease processes from
experts who know as much about that illness as anybody on the
earth. However, these specialists may know little more than you
about some common disease outside their own field.

The three clinical years will pass very quickly. Soon you will be
able to have the thrill of making your first correct diagnosis, of
assisting in the operating theatre and stitching wounds on a
Saturday night in the casualty department. The latter is an experience not to be missed. It may well be that as you pass from one
'firm' (a consultant plus his assistants) to another, you will come
across one particular line of medicine and this will fascinate you
more than anything else. This could be, for example, the study of
eye diseases (opthalmology), or dealing with sick children (paediat-
rics). This could lead you down the long pathway to becoming a

specialist. Or, you might find the whole course is interesting and feel that you would like to be a family doctor who treats patients with a variety of diseases from birth to grave.

As a clinical student, you will occasionally have the nerve-racking experience of taking a history and examining a patient under the full glare of the Professor, his assistants, nurses, and your fellow-students. This calls for a cool head and requires an element of showmanship in order to impress your chief. All the time, you will be frightened of missing some obvious sign of disease – to your lasting regret. I remember one unfortunate student who was asked to examine an abdomen in front of the Professor of Surgery and his retinue. We crowded into the room to hear the diagnosis. Understandably, the student was so nervous that he completely failed to notice the large abdominal swelling which everybody else could see with ease. All this sharpens the clinical acumen, as it is called. Although, as a student, your own ignorance can be exposed from time to time, and will be, you would be wise never to ask, at the bed-side, a question which your chief can't answer! Try to examine each patient 'blind', i.e. without knowing the diagnosis in advance.

The final examination will arrive sooner than you imagine and then you will be required to answer questions on almost any disease and make a diagnosis from hundreds of possibilities. All this comes with practice and you learn by your experiences and blunders in the wards and out-patient clinics. By now, you will have forgotten all about Advanced Level examinations and you will have to think hard to recall exactly what grades you obtained when you sat Advanced Level examinations, and to remember which questions you were asked when you went for your medical school interview. You might even have forgotten that you were helped by this book. One thing is certain, however. You will never regret the day that you obtained a place in medical school.

9
Final thoughts

From what you have already read in the earlier chapters, you will have concluded that you need to be industrious, self-disciplined, and informed if you are to commence training in medicine. The casual approach is only for the 'high-flier'. From reading this book so far, you will have become aware of the obstacles that lie between you and that medical school place. This last chapter contains miscellaneous additional information which may be useful to you. You are more likely to make a successful application if you are fully informed about the various medical schools.

THOSE ADVANCED LEVEL GRADES AGAIN

Many doctors believe that Advanced Level grades have become far too important in the selection procedure. Sadly, some deans are so impressed with intellectual brilliance that they seem to desire little else from new entrants to medical school. Undue emphasis on success in the physical sciences is helping to produce what one writer in the British Medical Journal has called a 'stranglehold' on the admissions procedure. Strangely, mathematics has become more important than the study of life itself – biology. Perhaps this is the result of the influence of the statistician on modern medical research. Certainly, a knowledge of pure and applied mathematics is about as much use to the average medical practitioner as would be a body-scanning machine to a first-aider. The raising of Advanced Level grades for admission to medical school is, in the author's opinion, giving an unfair advantage to those pupils who are privately educated since their schools will almost certainly place a greater emphasis on examination results. The medical profession and the general public would surely benefit if more students from the lower social classes were to enter medical school.

Your examiners at Advanced Level know that a badly set examination paper will prevent a healthy 'spread' of candidates' final marks. The outcome then is 'bunching' around the C grade level. This produces a situation where two pupils will be separated by only a few marks but by as much as *two* grades at Advanced Level. This must be an unsatisfactory situation, to say the least, for candidates and their teachers. It is fair to say that certain examination boards are very concerned about the need to 'stretch out' the range of marks in each grade, and they assure students that borderline cases have their papers re-marked very carefully. This may provide you with a crumb of comfort! If, when your results finally appear, you feel that you deserved a better grade (and especially if your teacher agrees with these sentiments) then you may apply through your school head teacher for a clerical check of your marks. This is usually done without charge. You can also request a re-mark but this could cost about £10–15 per subject at Advanced Level. One examination board recently received 945 requests for a re-mark at Advanced Level, but a mere 32 candidates obtained a change in their grade. So, don't build up your hopes in this direction. It must be added that the examining boards do their best to see that each examiner marks, as far as is humanly possible, to the same standard, every candidate's paper which he receives.

Entry to Scottish medical schools

Many candidates from England, Northern Ireland and Wales enter Scottish medical schools every year on the basis of their GCE Advanced Level results. Scottish applicants will enter through their results in the Higher Scottish Certificate of Education examinations. You should, of course, obtain the prospectuses and make a note of the examination requirements before you enter the name of a Scottish medical school on your UCCA form.

The University of St Andrews provides first and second MB courses only. Students then proceed to Manchester (usually) for the clinical part of the course.

The Queen's University of Belfast

About 6–800 students apply annually for the 155 places. The standard offer is ABB. The medical school caters primarily for Northern Ireland students and considers seriously only those applicants who place it as first or second choice on the UCCA form. The high grades probably deter many students from applying here.

BACK TO THE UCCA FORM AGAIN

Before you finally complete your UCCA application form, it would be wise to check with the dean of each of your five selected medical schools, not only what Advanced Level grades are currently requested for their standard conditional offer, but also the dean's UCCA form preference. The latter is very important. Don't, for example, waste your valuable fourth or fifth place on an 'independent' medical school (such as Southampton and Edinburgh) which expects nothing less than a first or second position on your UCCA form. On the other hand, Cardiff and Liverpool may still consider you although you have made them your fourth or fifth choice. Interestingly, one learned professor claims that he knows how to find the best candidates despite what position they have put his university on the UCCA form. This academic must be a genius. Beware of those medical schools who are unlikely to give you a second chance if you fail to obtain their requested GCE grades at your first attempt. Places like this include Liverpool, Dundee, Edinburgh and Aberdeen. They could leave you 'high and dry' if you fail and afterwards decide to re-apply to the original medical school which rejected you.

Normally, your five UCCA form choices will be for medicine, but certain medical schools, e.g. Southampton and Aberdeen, do not seem to object if you make pharmacy or biochemistry or similar, your fourth or fifth place on the UCCA form. This could give you a second string to your bow if you fail.

THOSE INTERVIEWS AGAIN

A recent television programme showed the great care with which the civil service mandarins of Whitehall select their successors, i.e. those who wish to become the 'Sir Humphreys' of tomorrow. Exhaustive interview procedures lasting two to three days, are standard practice. Medical school interviews, on the other hand, may be relatively brief and superficial and so you will have a very short period in which to impress your interviewers. It will be in the first couple of minutes of the interview that you will make your good impression or otherwise. 'Pull out all the stops', therefore, as soon as you enter the room. Probably this is the most important interview of your life. Make it clear that *you* have chosen to enter the medical profession and that you were uninfluenced by your parents, teachers or careers officer. Show by your answers that you want to study medicine and nothing else. Then, it will be difficult for the dean and his colleagues to ignore your youthful, unswerving enthusiasm. You may even remind them of their own zeal when they commenced studying medicine.

Your interviewers may be specialists in biochemistry or micro-biology and not medically qualified and 'care-orientated'. When aspiring medical students are asked their reasons for wanting to study medicine, they often reply 'I want to help people'. Try to avoid this over-worked expression. Why not declare an interest in one branch of medicine in which you have some knowledge, e.g. genetics, anaesthetics or surgery.

NO INTERVIEW . . .?

What can you do if you fail to obtain an interview after completing your UCCA form? Try writing a personal letter to the dean of your first and second choice, at least, and make out a good case for the medical school to at least see you in person and thereby appreciate what an excellent candidate you are! In this letter, it would be useful to reiterate your past examination successes, outside interests and strong reasons for wanting to apply to medical school. It would be useful if you could enclose with this letter a recent testimonial from somebody influential who is well acquainted with your own personal ability and strength of character. There is evidence that all this letter-writing can produce good results, sometimes.

Further reading

The following publications may help you to gather further information about applying to medical school, etc.

- *Entrance Requirements For Medical School*, published by The Secondary Heads Association, Chancery House, 107 St Paul's Road, Islington, London N1 2MB. Price of 1985 edition is £2.75. (This is invaluable.)

- *A Doctor .... Or Else?* by John Thurman. This book is especially useful if you are prepared to consider a career which is allied to the medical profession, e.g. radiography, pharmacy, etc. It is obtainable from Yare Valley Publishers, 20, Bluebell Road, Norwich. Tel (0603) 55329. It costs £3.80. Postage extra.

- *Learning Medicine* by Professor Peter Richards, Dean of Medicine at St Mary's Hospital Medical School. Obtainable from The British Medical Association, Tavistock Square, London WC1H 9JR. Price £4.00. Postage extra.

- *Degree Course Offers* by Brian Heap.

Entry data for United Kingdom medical schools

Tables 1 and 2 were originally published in *World Medicine* and are reproduced by kind permission of the former Editor of this magazine which no longer circulates. Table 1 shows entry data for the London Medical Schools, Table 2 shows entry data for the other medical schools in the United Kingdom (except Oxbridge). The figures have been brought up to date wherever possible. The author is grateful to those Deans who have kindly supplied the information.

If you are in doubt as to the current Advanced Level grades which are required by any particular medical school, then write personally to the dean and request the latest information. The numbers of applicants will vary from year to year.

Here are some extra details which could not be incorporated in the Tables:

- The Middlesex Medical School is being merged with the University College Hospital Medical School in October 1987. Admissions will be handled by University College. The exact number of applications which the combined Medical School will attract is unknown at present; it could be as much as 4000.

- King's College Medical School now gives preference to applicants who place it as choice 1–3 on the UCCA form. Incidentally, 'King's' produces an excellent prospectus.

- Liverpool makes offers around BBC/BBB to first-time applicants and ABB for those making a second application, (the 'A' must be

Table 1 Selection data for London medical schools

School	Places			Total applicants	Overseas	Mature	First MB course
	Total	Male	Female				
Guy's and St Thomas' (United) Medical School	195	112	83	1500 expected	5	12–15	No
Charing Cross and Westminster	155	87	68	2160	4	Up to 16	No
King's College	105	63	42	1112	2	10	No
The London	105	65	40	1600	6–8	3–6	No
The Royal Free	100	50	50	1600	2	7–10	No
St Bartholomew's	105	48	57	1100	2	11	No
St George's	151	83	68	2406	Up to 4	Up to 15	No
St Mary's	101	56	45	2392	Up to 3	8–10	No
University College and Middlesex	195	98	97	Probably 4000 +	5	25–30	No

Table 1 *contd*

School	Requested A Levels		Number interviewed	Length of interview (minutes)	Number of interviewers	Number of conditional and unconditional offers
	First time	Second time				
Guy's and St Thomas' (United) Medical School	BBB	Rarely considered	500	10–15	3	320
Charing Cross and Westminster	BBC	BBB or ABB	550	10–15	2–4	325
King's College	BBB	Virtually nil	320	10–15	3	265
The London	CCC	BBB	350	20	2	143
The Royal Free	BBC	ABB	450–500	15	5	240
St Bartholomew's	BBB	Variable	400	15	4	250
St George's	BBC	ABB	640	10–15	3–4	430
St Mary's	BCC	ABB	431	15	3	220
University College and Middlesex	CCC	BBB	450	15	3	See note in appendix 1

Table 2 Selection data for United Kingdom provincial medical schools (except Oxbridge)

School	Places Total	Places Male	Places Female	Total applicants	Overseas	Mature	First MB course
Aberdeen	134	69	65	1200	10	5	No
Belfast	150	95	55	750 – 800	Up to 20	5	Up to 5
Birmingham	163	78	85	1705	Up to 3	5–10	No
Bristol	120	59	61	1110	5–6	12–15	Up to 15
Cardiff	152	78	74	2000+	10	9–12	6
Dundee	121	74	47	1359	14	About 10	5–15
Edinburgh	185	93	92	1300+	2–10	5–10	5–10
Glasgow	225	118	107	1680	20	6–8	No
Leeds	160	89	71	2044	4–5	4–5	No
Leicester	120	56	64	1562	14	6	No
Liverpool	150	79	71	1950	7–8	6–12	No
Manchester	200	131	69	2195	Up to 20	10	Up to 15
Newcastle	140	65	75	1850	8–10	8–10	6–10
Nottingham	140	70	70	1700	12–15	2–6	No
Sheffield	130	65	65	2100	Up to 12	10	20
Southampton	135	76	64	1449	2	12	No

Table 2 *contd*

School	Requested A Levels		Number interviewed	Length of interview (minutes)	Number of interviewers	Number of conditional and unconditional offers
	First time	Second time				
Aberdeen	BBB	Variable	About 70	15	3	–
Belfast	AAB/ABB	AAB	Approx 50	15	1–2	400
Birmingham	BBB	AAA	558	15	3	346
Bristol	BBB	BBB	500	10–15	2	200
Cardiff	BBB	ABB	350	15	3	6–700
Dundee	BBC	No	About 30	30–45	2	248
Edinburgh	At least BBB	No	About 40	10–45	2	–
Glasgow	BBB	ABB/BBB	750	10–20	2	350
Leeds	BBB	ABB/Variable	About 50	20	2/3	850
Leicester	BBB	ABB	437	15–20	1	350
Liverpool	BBC/BBB	ABB	7–800	15	2	5–600
Manchester	BBB	AAA	100	30	2	600
Newcastle	BBB	ABB	500	15–20	2	200
Nottingham	BBB	ABB	400	15–20	3	250
Sheffield	BBB	ABB	425	15	1	400
Southampton	BBB	Rarely considered	150–180	15	2	240

obtained in chemistry.) Those who make a second application will be considered only if they have already obtained around 8 points on the A level scoring system at their first attempt. Candidates who re-sit must obtain all the A level grades at the same sitting.

- The first MB course is a useful entry point for students who have not obtained A levels in the science subjects required.

- The figure in the last column of the Tables may include some *unconditional* offers, i.e. offers to students who already possess the required Advanced level passes.

- If you are a particularly 'strong' candidate, you may get a conditional offer which is lower than the standard offer.

Addresses of medical schools in the United Kingdom and Southern Ireland

N.B. Medical schools are placed in alphabetical order according to the town in which they are located.

Aberdeen: The Registry Officer, Academic Section, University Office, University of Aberdeen, Regent Walk, Aberdeen AB9 1FX.

Belfast: The Dean, Faculty of Medicine, The Queen's University, Belfast BT7 1NN.

Birmingham: The Admissions Tutor, The Medical School, University of Birmingham, Birmingham B15 2TJ.

Bristol: Office of the Registrar, University of Bristol, Senate House, Tyndall Avenue, Bristol BS8 1TH.

Cambridge, pre-clinical: Cambridge Intercollegiate Admissions Office, Kellet Lodge, Tennis Court Road, Cambridge CB2 1QJ.

Cardiff: The Registrar, University of Wales College of Medicine, Heath Park, Cardiff CF4 4XN.

Cork, National University of Ireland: The Registrar, University College, Cork.

Dublin, Royal College of Surgeons in Ireland: The Dean and Registrar of the Medical School, 123, St. Stephen's Green, Dublin, 2.

Dublin, Trinity College: The Secretary, The Faculty of Medical Science, Trinity College, Dublin, 2.

Dublin, University College: The Dean, Faculty of Medicine, University College, Belfield, Dublin, 4.

Dundee: Faculty of Medicine, Level 10, Ninewells Hospital and Medical School, Dundee DD1 9SY.

Edinburgh: The Associate Dean, University of Edinburgh Medical School, Teviot Place, Edinburgh EH8 9AG.

Galway: Academic Secretary, University College, Galway.

Glasgow: The Convener, Medical Faculty Office, University of Glasgow, Glasgow G12 8QQ.

Leeds: Senior Administrative Officer, Faculty of Medicine, The University of Leeds, Leeds LS2 9JT.

Leicester: Senior Tutor, School of Medicine, The University, Leicester LE1 7RH.

Liverpool: Sub-Dean (Academic), Faculty of Medicine, Duncan Building, Royal Liverpool Hospital, PO Box 147, Liverpool, L69 3BX.

London, Guy's and St Thomas's Hospital, United Medical School: United Medical School of Guy's and St Thomas's Hospital, Lambeth Palace Road, London SE1 7EH.

London, Charing Cross and Westminster Medical School: Admissions Officer, Charing Cross and Westminster Medical School, The Reynolds Building, St Dunstan's Road, London W6 8RP.

London, King's College School of Medicine and Dentistry: The Secretary, King's College Hospital Medical School, Denmark Hill, London SE5 8RX.

London, London Hospital Medical School: Sub-Dean for Admissions, The London Hospital Medical School, Turner Street, London E1 2AD.

London, Royal Free Hospital School of Medicine: The Secretary, Royal Free Hospital School of Medicine, Rowland Hill Street, London NW3 2PF.

London, St Bartholomew's Hospital Medical College: The Dean, The Medical College of St Bartholomew's Hospital, West Smithfield, London EC1A 7BE.

London, St George's Hospital Medical School: The Secretary, St George's Hospital Medical School, Cranmer Terrace, Tooting, London SW17 0RG.

London, St Mary's Hospital Medical School: Admissions Secretary, St Mary's Hospital Medical School, Paddington, London W2 1PG.

London, University College and Middlesex School of Medicine: The Tutor, Faculty of Medical Sciences, Gower Street, London WC1E 6BT.

Manchester: Admissions Secretary, Faculty of Medicine, University of Manchester M13 9PL.

Newcastle: The Dean of Medicine, Medical School, The University, Newcastle-upon-Tyne NE2 4HH.

Nottingham: The Secretary, Faculty Office, The Medical School, Queen's Medical Centre, Nottingham NG7 2UH.

Oxford, pre-clinical: Oxford Colleges Admissions Office, University Offices, Wellington Square, Oxford OX1 2JO.

St Andrews: Admissions Officer for Medical Science Students, Faculty of Science, College Gate, St Andrews KY10 9AJ.

Sheffield: The Registrar, Faculty of Medicine, Beech Hill Road, Sheffield S10 2RX.

Southampton: The Dean, Faculty of Medicine, Southampton University, Bassett Crescent East, Southampton SO9 5NH.

Addresses of GCE examination boards

Associated Examining Board, Stag Hill House, University of Surrey, Guildford GU2 5XJ.

University of Cambridge Local Exams Syndicate, Syndicate Buildings, 17, Harvey Road, Cambridge CB1 2EU.

Joint Matriculation Board, Manchester M15 6EU.

London University Entrance and School Exams Council, University of London, 66–72, Gower Street, London WC1E 6EE.

Oxford Local Exams, Delegacy of Local Exams, Ewert Place, Banbury Road, Summertown, Oxford OX2 7BZ.

Southern Universities Joint Board for School Exams, Cotham Road, Bristol BS6 6DD.

Welsh Joint Education Committee, 245, Western Avenue, Cardiff CF5 2YX.

Northern Ireland Schools Exam Council, Beechill House, Beechill Road, Belfast BT8 4RS.

Oxford and Cambridge Board, 10, Trumpington Street, Cambridge CB2 1QB, or Elsfield Way, Oxford OX2 8EP.